THE
HEALING POWER
OF VINEGAR

Gayle Alleman, M.S., R.D.

Publications International, Ltd.

Chapter One
Versatile Vinegar's Rewards

Vinegar has long been valued for its healing properties, and it has found its way from the apothecary's shelf to the cook's pot. Today, vinegar continues to play a dual role, taking the place of less healthful dietary ingredients and helping to regulate blood sugar levels while entertaining our taste buds with its tart flavor.

There seems hardly an ailment that vinegar has not been touted to cure at some point in history. And while science has yet to prove the effectiveness of many of these folk cures, scores of people still praise and value vinegar as a healthful and healing food. So let's take a look at the history of vinegar, the healing claims made for it, and what science does and doesn't have to say about those claims. Along the way, we'll discover why vinegar deserves a place in every healthy kitchen.

Vinegar's Humble Beginnings

To understand the historical origins of vinegar, it helps to know a little something about how vinegar is "born." The following overview will help you understand the creation process, although you'll find a more detailed discussion of the many varieties of vinegar and how they are produced in chapter two.

EARLY WINES AND VINEGARS

Scientists believe wine originated during the Neolithic period (approximately 8500 B.C. to 4000 B.C., when humans first began farming and crafting stone tools) in Egypt and the Middle East. Large pottery jugs dating back to 6000 B.C. that were unearthed in archaeological digs possessed a strange yellow residue. Chemical analysis revealed the residue contained calcium tartrate, which is formed from tartaric acid, a substance that occurs naturally in large amounts only in grapes. So the traces strongly suggest the jugs were used to make or hold wine.

Considering the slow grape-pressing methods used at that time and the heat of the desert environment, grape juice would likely have fermented into wine quite quickly. Likewise, the wine would have turned to vinegar rapidly, if conditions were right.

So how did these ancient people—who had only recently (in evolutionary terms) begun planting their own food and fashioning tools—manage to understand and control fermentation enough to prevent all their wine from turning to vinegar before they could drink it? Based on evidence found in archaeological excavations, scientists believe that the first winemakers used jars with clay stoppers that helped control the fermentation process.

A complete analysis of the residue left in those ancient wine jugs also showed the presence of terebinth tree resin, which acts as a natural preservative and therefore would have helped slow the transformation of wine into vinegar. In Neolithic times, terebinth trees grew in the same area as grapes, and their berries and resin were harvested at the same time of year. So it's quite plausible that some of the berries or resins may have inadvertently become mixed with the grape harvest. Still unclear is whether the ancient wine-makers ever made the connection between the resins and the delayed conversion of wine into vinegar and began purposely adding the tree berries to their wine.

Vinegar is a dilute solution of acetic acid that results from a two-step fermentation process. The first step is the fermentation of sugar into alcohol, usually by yeast. Any natural source of sugar can be used. For example, the sugar may be derived from the juice, or cider, of fruit (such as grapes, apples, raisins, or even coconuts); from a grain (such as barley or rice); from honey, molasses, or sugar cane; or even, in the case of certain distilled vinegars, from the cellulose in wood (such as beech).

What you have at the end of this first phase, then, is an alcohol-containing liquid, such as wine (from grapes), beer (from barley), hard cider (from apples), or another fermented liquid. (The alcoholic liquid used to create a vinegar is generally reflected in the vinegar's name—for example, red wine vinegar, white wine vinegar, malt vinegar, or cider vinegar.)

In the second phase of the vinegar-production process, certain naturally occurring bacteria known as acetobacters combine the alcohol-containing liquid with oxygen to form the acetic-acid solution we call vinegar. Acetic acid is what gives vinegar its sour taste. Although time-consuming, this second phase of the process will happen without human intervention if the alcoholic liquid is exposed to oxygen long enough.

Thus, it is not surprising that the first vinegar was the result of an ancient accident. Once upon a time, a keg of wine (presumably a poorly sealed one that allowed oxygen in) was stored too long, and when the would-be drinkers opened it, they found a sour liquid instead of wine. The name "vinegar" is derived from the French words for "sour wine."

Fortunately, our resourceful ancestors found ways to use the "bad" wine. They put it to work as a cure-all, a food preservative, and later, a flavor enhancer. It wasn't long before they figured out how to make vinegar on purpose, and producing it became one of the world's earliest commercial industries.

The use of vinegar as medicine probably started soon after it was discovered. Its healing virtues are extolled in records of the Babylonians, and the great Greek physician Hippocrates reportedly used it as an antibiotic. Ancient Greek doctors poured vinegar into wounds and over dressings as a disinfectant, and they gave concoctions of honey and vinegar to patients recovering from illness. In Asia, early samurai warriors believed vinegar to be a tonic that would increase their strength and vitality.

Vinegar has continued to be used as a medicine in more recent times. During the Civil War and World War I, for example, military medics used vinegar to treat wounds. And folk traditions around the world still espouse vinegar for a wide variety of ailments. Natural-healing enthusiasts and vinegar fans continue to honor and use many of those folk remedies.

A CORNUCOPIA OF CLAIMS

The folk- and natural-healing claims made for vinegar through the ages have been plentiful and varied. Even in the current era of high-tech medicine, some proponents of natural healing still encourage traditional uses of vinegar. They have also added certain newly recognized or newly defined (within the past hundred years or so, that is) medical conditions to the list of health concerns for which they recommend vinegar.

Other present-day vinegar fans view it as an overall health-boosting, disease-fighting tonic and recommend mixing a teaspoon or tablespoon of cider vinegar with a glass of water and drinking it each morning or before meals. (Apple cider vinegar is the traditional vinegar of choice for home or folk remedies, although some recent claims have been made for the benefits of wine vinegars, especially red wine vinegar. Unless otherwise specified, though, the vinegar we'll be referring to in the rest of this chapter is apple cider vinegar.)

Perhaps most amazingly, vinegar is heralded as a potential healer of many of today's most common serious ailments. Devotees believe vinegar can help prevent or heal heart disease, diabetes, obesity, cancer, aging-related ailments, and a host of other conditions. They say it is full of vitamins, minerals, fiber, enzymes, and pectin and often attribute vinegar's medicinal effects to the presence of these ingredi-

VINEGAR TO THE RESCUE?

Apple cider vinegar has long been touted as a natural remedy for an amazing array of ailments, although there's little hard scientific evidence available to support many of its purported healing benefits. Vinegar has been used to treat the following conditions through the ages:

INTERNAL USES

appetite and digestive problems
asthma
constipation
cough and colds
depression
diarrhea
dizziness
fatigue
food poisoning
gallstones and kidney stones
headache
heartburn and hiccups
high blood cholesterol
high blood pressure
kidney and bladder problems
metabolism problems
osteoporosis
poor blood clotting
poor circulation
sore throat
upset stomach
urinary tract infections
yeast infections

EXTERNAL USES

age spots and liver spots
athlete's foot
dandruff
dry hair
ear infections and
   blockages
hay fever
hearing problems
insect stings and bites
insomnia
joint pain
leg cramps
nasal congestion
skin problems, such as
   eczema and rashes
strained muscles
sunburn
tired, sore eyes

ents. The following are some of the specific claims made for apple cider vinegar:

◆ **It reduces blood cholesterol levels and heart-disease risk.** Apple cider vinegar fans say it contains pectin, which attaches to cholesterol and carries it out of the body, thus decreasing the risk of heart disease. In addition, many vinegar proponents say it is high in potassium, and high-potassium foods play a role in reducing the risk of heart disease by helping to prevent or lower high blood pressure. Calcium is also an important nutrient for keeping blood pressure in check, and as you will learn shortly, vinegar is sometimes promoted as having a high calcium content. Many also claim vinegar helps the body absorb this essential mineral from other foods in the diet.

◆ **It treats diabetes.** Apple cider vinegar may help control blood sugar levels, which helps to ward off diabetes complications, such as nerve damage and blindness. It also might help prevent other serious health problems, such as heart disease, that often go hand-in-hand with diabetes.

◆ **It fights obesity and aids in weight loss.** Some marketers proclaim that apple cider vinegar is high in fiber and therefore aids in weight loss. (Fiber provides bulk but is indigestible by the body, so foods high in fiber provide a feeling of fullness for fewer calories.) A daily dose is also said to control or minimize the appetite. (Ironically, some folk traditions advise taking apple cider vinegar before a meal for the opposite effect—to stimulate the appetite in people who have lost interest in eating.)

◆ **It prevents cancer and aging.** Apple cider vinegar proponents declare it contains high levels of the antioxidant beta-carotene (a form of vitamin A) and therefore helps prevent cancer and the ill effects of aging. (Antioxidants help protect the body's cells against damage from unstable molecules called free radicals; free-radical damage has been linked to various conditions, including coronary heart disease, cancer, and the aging process.)

- ◆ **It prevents osteoporosis.** Advocates say apple cider vinegar releases calcium and other minerals from the foods you eat so your body is better able to absorb and use them to strengthen bones. Vinegar allegedly allows the body to absorb one-third more calcium from green vegetables than it would without the aid of vinegar. Some fans also say apple cider vinegar is itself a great source of calcium.

Based on these claims, apple cider vinegar certainly seems to be a wonder food. And it's understandably tempting to *want* to believe that some food or drug or substance will make diabetes, obesity, cancer, and osteoperosis go away with little or no discomfort, effort, or risk.

However, as a wise consumer, you know that when something sounds too good to be true, it almost certainly is. So when it comes to your health—especially when you're dealing with such major medical conditions—it's important to take a step back and look carefully at the evidence.

A Closer Look at the Claims

With such dramatic claims made for it, you would think that vinegar would be high on the lists of medical researchers searching for the next breakthrough. Yet in the past 20 years, there has been very little research into the use of vinegar for therapeutic health purposes.

Granted, a lack of supporting scientific research is a common problem with many natural and alternative therapies.

COMPLEMENTARY RESEARCH PRIORITIES

The Naional Center for Complementary and Alternative Medicine (NCCAM) studies substances that hold possible promise in treating a health condition because they exhibit some type of active compound. An active compound can be a vitamin, mineral, or phytochemical—anything in a food, herb, or other natural substance that has some kind of therapeutic effect on the body.

The organization's list of research topics includes cardiovascular disease, disorders of the digestive tract, respiratory diseases (including colds and asthma), and obesity.

But even the National Center for Complementary and Alternative Medicine (NCCAM), a division of the U.S. government's National Institutes of Health that was created specifically to investigate natural or unconventional therapies that hold promise, has not published any studies about vinegar, despite the fact that there has been renewed interest in vinegar's healing benefits recently.

So without solid scientific studies, can we judge whether vinegar provides the kinds of dramatic benefits that its promoters and fans attribute to it? Not conclusively. But we can look at the claims and compare them to the little scientific knowledge we do have about vinegar.

Those who have faith in apple cider vinegar as a wide-ranging cure say its healing properties come from an abundance of nutrients that remain after apples are fermented to make apple cider vinegar. They contend that vinegar is rich in minerals and vitamins, including calcium, potassium, and beta-carotene; complex carbohydrates and fiber, including the soluble fiber pectin; amino acids (the building blocks of protein); beneficial enzymes; and acetic acid (which gives vinegar its taste).

These substances do play many important roles in health and healing, and some are even considered essential nutrients for human health. The problem is that standard nutritional analysis of vinegar, including apple cider vinegar, has not shown it to be a good source of most of these substances.

Take a look at the table on the next two pages—it shows the results of a nutritional analysis of an apple compared with the nutritional breakdown of two different amounts of apple cider vinegar. One tablespoon of apple cider vinegar per day is the typical therapeutic dose recommended, so the nutrients found in this amount of the vinegar are shown in the second column of the table. Just to be sure that the small amount of vinegar in a tablespoon isn't the sole explanation for the apparent lack of nutrients, the table also includes the nutritional analysis of a larger amount (half a cup) of vinegar. You'll notice that even at that higher dose, vinegar does not appear to include significant amounts of most of the nutrients that are claimed to be the source of its medicinal value.

To put all this information into some context, the column at the far right in the table shows the daily amounts needed by a typical adult who consumes 2,000 calories per day. (Requirements haven't been established for some of the other substances that are often cited as contributing to vinegar's beneficial effects.)

As you can see, the one milligram of calcium in one table-spoon of apple cider vinegar does not come close to the 300 milligrams of calcium in eight ounces of milk, as some promoters of apple cider vinegar claim. In fact, it supplies only a tiny fraction of the 1,000 milligrams a typical adult needs in a day. Vinegar also contains little potassium.

In terms of pectin, the type of soluble fiber that is said to bind to cholesterol and help carry it out of the body, apple cider vinegar contains no measurable amounts of it or of

Nutrient	One medium apple, raw (2¾ inch diameter)	1 Tbsp. apple cider vinegar	½ cup apple cider vinegar	Daily amount needed by avg. adult
Calories	72	3	25	2,000
Carbohydrate	19.06 g	0.14 g	1.11 g	130 g
Fat	0.23 g	0 g	0 g	65 g (max.)
Protein	0.36 g	0 g	0 g	46 g (women) 56 g (men)
Fiber	3.3 g	0 g	0 g	25 g (women) 38 g (men)
Minerals				
Calcium	8 mg	1 mg	8 mg	1,000 mg
Iron	0.17 mg	0.03 mg	0.24 mg	18 mg (women) 8 g (men)

any other type of fiber. So it would seem that pectin could not account for any cholesterol-binding activity that vinegar might be shown to have.

Do apple cider vinegar's secrets lie in the vitamins it contains? No. According to the USDA, apple cider vinegar contains no vitamin A, vitamin B6, vitamin C, vitamin E,

Nutrient	One medium apple, raw (2¾ inch diameter)	1 Tbsp. apple cider vinegar	½ cup apple cider vinegar	Daily amount needed by avg. adult
Magnesium	7 mg	1 mg	6 mg	320 mg (women) 420 mg (men)
Phosphorus	15 mg	1 mg	10 mg	700 mg
Potassium	148 mg	11 mg	87 mg	4,700 mg
Sodium	1 mg	1 mg	6 mg	1,500 mg
Zinc	0.06 mg	0.01 mg	0.05 mg	8 mg (women) 11 mg (men)
Copper	0.037 mg	0.001 mg	0.01 mg	0.9 mg
Manganese	0.048 mg	0.037 mg	0.298 mg	1.8 mg (women) 2.3 mg (men)
Selenium	0 mcg	0 mcg	0.1 mcg	55 mcg

Source: U.S. Department of Agriculture, Agricultural Research Service. 2005. USDA National Nutrient Database for Standard Reference, Release 18. Nutrient Data Laboratory Home Page, www.ars.usda.gov/ba/bhnrc/ndl. Note: g = grams, mg = milligrams, mcg = micrograms.

vitamin K, thiamin, riboflavin, niacin, pantothenic acid, or folate.

What about some of the other health-boosting substances that are alleged to be in vinegar? According to detailed nutritional analyses, apple cider vinegar contains no significant amounts of amino acids. Nor does it contain ethyl alcohol, caffeine, theobromine, beta-carotene, alpha-carotene, beta-cryptoxanthin, lycopene, lutein, or zeaxanthin.

HOW VINEGAR *CAN* HELP

So if vinegar doesn't actually contain all the substances that are supposed to account for its medicinal benefits, does that mean it has no healing powers? Hardly. As mentioned, so little research has been done on vinegar that we can't totally rule out many of the dramatic claims made for it. Although we know vinegar doesn't contain loads of nutrients traditionally associated with good health, it may well contain yet-to-be-identified phytochemicals (beneficial compounds in plants) that would account for some of the healing benefits that vinegar fans swear by. Scientists continue to discover such beneficial substances in all kinds of foods.

But beyond that possibility, there appear to be more tangible and realistic—albeit less sensational—ways that vinegar can help the body heal. Rather than being the dramatic blockbuster cure that we are endlessly (and fruitlessly) searching for, vinegar seems quite capable of playing myriad supporting roles—as part of an overall lifestyle approach—that can help us fight serious health conditions, such as osteoporosis, diabetes, and heart disease.

REMEDIES FOR MINOR AILMENTS

Vinegar's potential for treating or preventing major medical problems is of interest to almost everyone. But it also has been cherished as a home remedy for some common minor ailments for centuries. Although they're not life-or-death issues, these minor health problems can be uncomfortable, and there is often little modern medicine can offer in the way of a cure. So you may want to give vinegar a shot to determine for yourself if it can help. (It's always best when trying any remedy for the first time to run it past your doctor to be sure there is no reason you should not try it.)

Stomach upset. To settle minor stomach upset, try a simple cider vinegar tonic with a meal. Drinking a mixture of a spoonful of vinegar in a glass of water is said to improve digestion and ease minor stomach upset by stimulating digestive juices.

Common cold symptoms. Apple cider vinegar is also an age-old treatment for symptoms of the common cold. For a sore throat, mix one teaspoon of apple cider vinegar into a glass of water; gargle with a mouthful of the solution and then swallow it, repeating until you've finished all the solution in the glass. For a natural cough syrup, mix half a tablespoon apple cider vinegar with half a tablespoon honey and swallow. Finally, you can add a quarter-cup of apple cider vinegar to the recommended amount of water in your room vaporizer to help with congestion.

Continued on page 16

Itching or stinging from minor insect bites. In the folk medicine of New England, rural Indiana, and parts of the Southwest, a vinegar wash is sometimes used for treating bites and stings. (However, if the person bitten has a known allergy to insect venom or begins to exhibit signs of a serious allergic reaction, such as widespread hives, swelling of the face or mouth, difficulty breathing, or loss of consciousness, skip the home remedies and seek immediate medical attention.) Pour undiluted vinegar over the bite or sting, avoiding surrounding healthy skin as much as possible. Or, use vinegar mixed with cornstarch to make a paste. Apply paste to a bee sting or bug bite and let dry.

Athlete's foot. One way to eliminate athlete's foot (or other fungal infections) is to create an environment that is inhospitable to the fungus that causes the condition. The Amish traditionally use a footbath of vinegar and water to discourage the growth of athlete's foot fungus. To try this remedy, mix one cup of vinegar into two quarts of water in a basin or pan. Soak your feet in this solution every night for 15 to 30 minutes, using a fresh solution each night. Or, if you prefer, mix up a solution using one cup of vinegar and one cup of water. Apply the solution to the affected parts of your feet with a cotton ball. Let your feet dry completely before putting on socks and/or shoes.

INCREASING CALCIUM ABSORPTION

If there is one thing vinegar fans, marketers, alternative therapists, and scientists alike can agree on, it's that vinegar is high in acetic acid. And acetic acid, like other acids, can increase the body's absorption of important minerals from the foods we eat. Therefore, including apple cider vinegar in meals or possibly even drinking a mild tonic of vinegar and water (up to a tablespoon of vinegar in a glass of water) just before or with meals might improve your body's ability to absorb the essential minerals locked in foods.

Vinegar may be especially useful to women, who generally have a hard time getting all the calcium their bodies need to keep bones strong and prevent the debilitating, bone-thinning disease osteoporosis. Although dietary calcium is most abundant in dairy products such as milk, many women (and men) suffer from a condition called lactose intolerance that makes it difficult or impossible for them to digest the sugar in milk. As a result, they may suffer uncomfortable gastrointestinal symptoms, such as cramping and diarrhea, when they consume dairy products. These women must often look elsewhere to fulfill their dietary calcium needs.

Dark, leafy greens are good sources of calcium, but some of these greens also contain compounds that inhibit calcium absorption. Fortunately for dairy-deprived women (and even those who do drink milk), a few splashes of vinegar or a tangy vinaigrette on their greens may very well allow them to absorb more valuable calcium.

CONTROLLING BLOOD SUGAR LEVELS

Vinegar has recently won attention for its potential to help people with type 2 diabetes get a better handle on their disease. Improved control could help them delay or prevent such complications as blindness, impotence, and a loss of feeling in the extremities that may necessitate amputation. Also, because people with diabetes are at increased risk for other serious health problems, such as heart disease, improved control of their diabetes could potentially help to ward off these associated conditions, as well.

With type 2 diabetes, the body's cells become resistant to the action of the hormone insulin. The body normally releases insulin into the bloodstream in response to a meal. Insulin's job is to help the body's cells take in the glucose, or sugar, from the carbohydrates in food, so they can use it for energy. But when the body's cells become insulin resistant, the sugar from food begins to build up in the blood, even while the cells themselves are starving for it. (High levels of insulin tend to build up in the blood, too, because the body releases more and more insulin to try to transport the large amounts of sugar out of the bloodstream and into the cells.)

Over time, high levels of blood sugar can damage nerves throughout the body and otherwise cause irreversible harm. So one major goal of diabetes treatment is to normalize blood sugar levels and keep them in a healthier range as much as possible. And that's where vinegar appears to help.

It seems that vinegar may be able to inactivate some of the digestive enzymes that break the carbohydrates from food into sugar, thus slowing the absorption of sugar from a meal into the bloodstream. Slowing sugar absorption gives the insulin-resistant body more time to pull sugar out of the blood and thus helps prevent the blood sugar level from rising so high. Blunting the sudden jump in blood sugar that would usually occur after a meal also lessens the amount of insulin the body needs to release at one time to remove the sugar from the blood.

A study cited in 2004 in the American Diabetes Association's publication *Diabetes Care* indicates that vinegar holds real promise for helping people with diabetes. In the study, 21 people with either type 2 diabetes or insulin resistance (a prediabetic condition) and 8 control subjects were each given a solution containing five teaspoons of vinegar, five teaspoons of water, and one teaspoon of saccharin two minutes before ingesting a high-carbohydrate meal. The blood sugar and insulin levels of the participants were measured before the meal and 30 minutes and 60 minutes after the meal.

Vinegar increased overall insulin sensitivity 34 percent in the study participants who were insulin-resistant and 19 percent in those with type 2 diabetes. That means their bodies actually became more receptive to insulin, allowing the hormone to do its job of getting sugar out of the blood and into the cells. Both blood sugar and blood insulin levels were lower than usual in the insulin-resistant participants, which is more good news. Surprisingly, the control group (who had neither diabetes nor a prediabetic condition but were given the vinegar solution) also experienced a reduction in insulin levels in the blood. These findings are significant because, in addition to the nerve damage caused by perpetually elevated blood sugar levels, several chronic conditions, including heart disease, have been linked to excess insulin in the blood over prolonged periods of time.

More studies certainly need to be done to confirm the extent of vinegar's benefits for type 2 diabetes patients and those at risk of developing this increasingly common disease. But for now, people with type 2 diabetes might be wise to talk with their doctors or dietitians about consuming more vinegar.

REPLACING UNHEALTHY FATS AND SODIUM

As you'll discover in chapter two, there are some delicious varieties of vinegar available. Each bestows a different taste or character on foods. The diversity and intensity of flavor are key to one important healing role that vinegar can play. Whether you are trying to protect yourself from cardiovascular diseases, such as heart disease, high blood pressure, or stroke, or you have been diagnosed with one or more of these conditions and have been advised to clean up your diet, vinegar should become a regular cooking and dining companion. That's because a tasty vinegar can often be used in place of sodium and/or ingredients high in saturated or *trans* fats to add flavor and excitement to a variety of dishes.

Saturated and *trans* fats have been shown to have a detrimental effect on blood cholesterol levels (see page 22 for a more detailed discussion of the link between these fats and high blood cholesterol levels), and experts recommend that people who have or are at risk of developing high blood pressure cut back on the amount of sodium they consume. Using vinegar as a simple, flavorful substitute for these less healthful ingredients as often as possible can help people manage blood cholesterol and blood pressure levels and, in turn, help ward off heart disease and stroke.

You'll find detailed advice about including more vinegar in your diet in chapter two. But the following suggestions will give you some sense of how vinegar can help you create and enjoy a diet that may lower your blood cholesterol and blood pressure and decrease your risks of heart disease and stroke:

◆ Make a vinegar-based coleslaw rather than a creamy, mayonnaise-based one. Because mayonnaise is made up almost completely of unhealthy fats and cholesterol, this easy switch can dramatically reduce the cholesterol and fat in this popular side dish.

◆ Enjoy healthier fish and chips. Instead of dipping fish in tartar sauce and drenching fries in salt and ketchup, splash them with a little malt vinegar. (Also consider baking the fish and the potatoes instead of frying them.) Because it contains mayonnaise, tartar sauce is high in unhealthy fats and cholesterol.

◆ Use vinegar-based salad dressings instead of creamy, mayonnaise-based dressings. Choose or make a flavorful herb salad dressing that contains mostly water, vinegar, and just a touch of oil to help it adhere to your salad veggies.

◆ Opt for vinegar instead of mayonnaise or other common, bad-fat-laden sandwich spreads to add flavor and moisture to sandwiches.

◆ When making a dish that contains beans, add a little vinegar near the end of cooking—it will dramatically decrease the amount of salt you'll need. It perks up the flavor of beans without raising your blood pressure.

◆ You can also use vinegar as a tangy marinade for tenderizing less-fatty cuts of meat. Choosing meat with less fat on the edges and less marbling within is one of the easiest ways to trim unhealthy fats from your diet. Unfortunately, meats that don't have as much marbling tend to be a little tougher. So vinegar can do double duty by adding a dash of zing as it tenderizes.

TARGET: SATURATED AND TRANS FATS

Any help that vinegar can provide in reducing the deleterious effects of saturated and *trans* fats will be a boon to your health.

Saturated fat. This fat is unhealthy because the body turns it into artery-clogging cholesterol, which is harmful to your heart. Saturated fat is mostly found in animal products and is solid at room temperature. It is the white fat you see along the edge or marbled throughout a piece of meat, and it is in the skin of poultry. It is also "hidden" in whole milk and foods made from whole milk, as well as in tropical oils such as coconut oil. Dietitians recommend that you eat only small amounts of saturated fat.

Trans *fat*. *Trans* fat is the most harmful type of fat, and you should try to avoid it. Most *trans* fat is manufactured by forcing hydrogen into liquid polyunsaturated fat. The process, called hydrogenation, can create a solid fat product; margarine is made this way. Hydrogenation gives foods that contain *trans* fat a longer shelf life and helps stabilize their flavors, but your body pays a big price. The body recognizes *trans* fat as being saturated and converts it to cholesterol, which raises LDL levels and lowers HDL levels. What's worse is that, unlike saturated fat, *trans* fat disrupts cell membranes. Cell membranes are comprised of uniformly configured fatty acid chains that are linked together through tight chemical bonds. When *trans* fat works its way into the chains, it alters these bonds and creates "leaks" in the cell membrane. This upsets the flow of nutrients and waste products into and out of the cell and may be linked to reduced immune function and possibly cancer.

MAKING A HEALTHY DIET EASIER TO SWALLOW

Some of our strongest natural weapons against cancer and aging are fruits and vegetables. The antioxidants and phyto-chemicals they contain seem to hold real promise in lowering our risk of many types of cancer. Their antioxidants also help to protect cells from the free-radical damage that is thought to underlie many of the changes we associate with aging. Protected cells don't wear out and need replacing as often as cells that aren't bathed in antioxidants. Scientists think this continual cell replacement may be at the root of aging.

The U.S. Department of Agriculture's (USDA) 2005 Dietary Guidelines recommend that the average person eat about two cups of fruit and two-and-a-half cups of vegetables every day. One way to add excitement and variety to all those vegetables is to use vinegar liberally as a seasoning.

◆ Rice vinegar and a little soy sauce give veggies an Asian flavor or can form the base of an Asian coleslaw.

◆ Red wine vinegar or white wine vinegar can turn boring vegetables into a quick-and-easy marinated-vegetable salad that's ready to be grabbed out of the refrigerator whenever hunger strikes. Just chop your favorite veggies, put them in a bowl with a marinade of vinegar, herbs, and a dash of olive oil, and let them sit for at least an hour. (You don't need much oil to make the marinade stick to the veggies, so go light, and be sure you choose olive oil.)

◆ Toss chopped vegetables in a vinegar-and-olive-oil salad dressing before loading them on skewers and putting them on the backyard grill. The aroma and flavor will actually have your family asking for sec-onds—*of vegetables!*

THE TRUTH ABOUT VINEGAR SUPPLEMENTS

Some people believe in the healing power of apple cider vinegar but would rather take it in tablet form instead of using it as a daily tonic or adding it to food. But like any shortcut on the road to better health, you can't be sure this one will get you to the goal you're aiming for.

Part of the reason for concern is that the U.S. Food and Drug Administration (FDA) does not regulate supplements, so you really can't be sure what you're getting. In a study reported in the July 2005 *Journal of the American Dietetic Association*, for example, researchers analyzed eight different brands of apple cider vinegar tablets. The analysis showed most had acetic acid levels different from those claimed on the label. How much of a problem is this? Well, it would be natural to think the more acetic acid the better. But in truth, at a level of 11 percent, acetic acid can cause burns to the skin. And at 20 percent, it is considered poisonous.

Some of the analyzed supplements, however, claimed to contain a frightening 35 percent acetic acid! Fortunately for their users, none did. The acetic acid content actually ranged from 1.04 percent to 10.57 percent. Another reason to go natural: Several of the samples were contaminated with mold and/or yeast, including one that claimed to be yeast-free.

In addition, because so little scientific research has been done to verify the healing claims made for vinegar—and the possible ingredients or actions that might be responsible—it's impossible to know if supplements would have the same effects as the real thing. Indeed, most of vinegar's benefits—at least the ones that rest on the most solid scientific grounds—are those based on its use as a substitute for unhealthy ingredients in the diet, a role that simply could not be played by a pill.

So at this time, it would seem you are almost certainly better off including more vinegar in your diet, taking advantage of its potential healing benefits as well as its phenomenal flavors, rather than spending more money on supplements that may not have any benefit and could even be dangerous.

◆ After steaming vegetables, drizzle a little of your favorite vinegar over them instead of adding butter or salt. They'll taste so good, you may never get to the meat on your plate.

By enhancing the flavor of vegetables with vinegar, you and your family will be inclined to eat more of them. And that—many researchers and doctors would agree—will likely go a long way toward protecting your body's cells from the damage that can lead to cancer and other problems of aging.

REMOVING HARMFUL SUBSTANCES FROM PRODUCE

Some people are concerned that eating large amounts of fruits and vegetables may lead to an unhealthy consump-

ADD FLAVOR, NOT CALORIES

Vinegar contains very few calories—only 25 in half a cup! Compare that to the nearly 800 calories you get in half a cup of mayonnaise, and you have a real fat-fighting food. So if you're looking to lose weight, using vinegar in place of mayonnaise whenever you can will help you make a serious dent in your calorie (and fat) intake.

Vinegar can also help you have your dessert and cut calories, too. Use a splash of balsamic vinegar to bring out the sweetness and flavor of strawberries without any added sugar. Try it on other fruits that you might sprinkle sugar on—you'll be pleasantly surprised at the difference a bit of balsamic vinegar can make. And for a real unexpected treat on a hot summer evening, drizzle balsamic vinegar—instead of high-fat, sugary caramel or chocolate sauce—on a dish of reduced-fat vanilla ice cream. Can't imagine that combination? Just try it.

tion of pesticides and other farm-chemical residues. Vinegar can lend a hand here, too. Washing produce in a mixture of water and vinegar appears to help remove certain pesticides, according to the small amount of research that has been published. Vinegar also appears to be helpful in getting rid of harmful bacteria on fruits and vegetables.

To help remove potentially harmful residues, mix a solution of 10 percent vinegar to 90 percent water (for example, mix one cup of white vinegar in nine cups of water). Then, place produce in the vinegar solution, let it soak briefly, and then swish it around in the solution. Finally, rinse the produce thoroughly.

Do not use this process on tender, fragile fruits, such as berries, that might be damaged in the process or soak up too much vinegar through their porous skins.

Some pesticide residues are trapped beneath the waxy coatings that are applied to certain vegetables to help them retain moisture. The vinegar solution probably won't wash those pesticides away, so peeling lightly may be a better option. Some research suggests that cooking further eliminates some pesticide residue.

THE SOUR THAT'S REALLY SWEET

Much more research needs to be done to investigate all of vinegar's healing potential. But even with the evidence available, it's clear that vinegar holds some healing powers. It is not a too-good-to-be-true miracle cure, but it can be used in a variety of ways to enhance your efforts to fight serious, chronic diseases (and as noted in the box on pages 15 and 16, it may lend a healing hand against some common, minor discomforts).

In that sense, vinegar is like many of the other lifestyle adjustments, drugs, and therapies used in our battles against common, chronic, and often life-threatening diseases: It is just one of a variety of important steps that can help us defend ourselves. But unlike many of the other elements that go into treating or preventing disease, vinegar is one you'll certainly enjoy incorporating into your life. In chapter two, you'll find the practical information you need to make vinegar a staple of your healing kitchen.

Body Beautiful

Vinegar is a wonderful—and inexpensive—addition to your beauty regimen. It can help restore the natural acidity to your skin, which may clear up skin problems such as dryness, iching, flaking, and acne. Here are some beauty tips and tricks that will help you look great without spending a fortune.

Itchy skin. To relieve itchy skin and/or aching muscles, add eight ounces apple cider vinegar to a bathtub of warm water. Soak in tub for at least 15 minutes.

Cleansers and toners. Use a mixture of half vinegar, half water to clean your face. Then rinse with vinegar diluted with water, and let your face air-dry to seal in moisture.

Conditioning. Vinegar is a great hair conditioner and can improve cleanliness and shine. For simple conditioning, just add one tablespoon vinegar to your hair as you rinse it.

Dandruff. Massage full-strength vinegar into your scalp several times a week before shampooing. This can help create healthy hair and control dandruff.

Age spots. Vinegar mixed with onion juice may help reduce the appearance of age spots. Mix equal parts of onion juice and vinegar, and dab onto age spots. After several weeks of this routine, spots should lighten.

Scrub. Clean very dirty hands by scrubbing with cornmeal that has been moistened with a little bit of apple cider vinegar. Rinse in cool water, then dry.

Aftershave. Apple cider vinegar is a great aftershave for men that will keep their skin soft and young looking. Keep a small bottle of it in the medicine cabinet, and splash on your face after shaving.

VINEGAR QUOTABLES

"Men are like wine—some turn to vinegar, but the best improve with age."

–Pope John XXIII (1881–1963)

"As the best wine doth make the sharpest vinegar, so the deepest love turneth to the deadliest hate."

–John Lyly (English writer, 1553–1606)

"To make a good salad is to be a brilliant diplomatist—the problem is entirely the same in both cases. To know exactly how much oil one must put with one's vinegar."

–Oscar Wilde (Irish writer, 1854–1900)

Chapter Two
VINEGAR IN THE KITCHEN

With a splash here or a half-cup there, vinegar adds zing and zest to your cooking and brings out the flavors of other foods. No kitchen pantry is complete without at least a few different types of this flavor-enhancer. Vinegar is a must-have ingredient for vinaigrettes, marinades, food preservation, or any recipe that needs a little extra kick.

You might be surprised to learn that there are dozens of types of vinegar. The most common vinegars found in American kitchens are white distilled and apple cider, but the more adventurous may also use red wine vinegar, white wine vinegar, rice vinegar, or gourmet varieties, such as 25-year-old balsamic vinegar or rich black fig vinegar.

As you've learned, vinegar can be made from just about any food that contains natural sugars. Yeast ferments these sugars into alcohol, and certain types of bacteria convert that alcohol a second time into vinegar. A weak acetic acid remains after this second fermentation; the acid has flavors reminiscent of the original fermented food, such as apples or grapes. Acetic acid is what gives vinegar its distinct tart taste.

Pure acetic acid can be made in a laboratory; when diluted with water, it is sometimes sold as white vinegar. However, acetic acids created in labs lack the subtle flavors found in true vinegars, and synthesized versions don't hold a candle to vinegars fermented naturally from summer's sugar-laden fruits or other foods.

Vinegars can be made from many different foods that add their own tastes to the final products, but additional ingredients, such as herbs, spices, or fruits, can be added for further flavor enhancement.

VINEGAR VARIETIES

Vinegar is great for a healthy, light style of cooking. The tangy taste often reduces the need for salt, especially in soups and bean dishes. It can also cut the fat in a recipe because it balances flavors without requiring the addition of as much cream, butter, or oil. Vinegar flavors range from mild to bold, so you're sure to find one with the taste you want. A brief look at some of the various vinegars available may help you choose a new one for your culinary escapades.

WHITE VINEGAR

This clear variety is the most common type of vinegar in American households. It is made either from grain-based ethanol or laboratory-produced acetic acid and then diluted with water. Its flavor is a bit too harsh for most cooking uses, but it is good for pickling and performing many cleaning jobs around the house.

APPLE CIDER VINEGAR

Apple cider vinegar is the second-most-common type of vinegar in the United States. This light-tan vinegar made from apple cider adds a tart and subtle fruity flavor to your cooking. Apple cider vinegar is best for salads, dressings, marinades, condiments, and most general vinegar needs.

WINE VINEGAR

This flavorful type of vinegar is made from a blend of either red wines or white wines and is common in Europe, especially Germany. Creative cooks often infuse wine vinegars with extra flavor by tucking in a few sprigs of well-washed fresh herbs, dried herbs, or fresh berries. Red wine vinegar is often flavored with natural raspberry flavoring, if not with the fruit itself.

PASTEURIZED FOR YOUR PROTECTION

Some apple cider vinegars proudly proclaim to be "raw, organic, and unpasteurized," but beware: Buying an unpasteurized product is risky business.

Most apple cider is made from apples that have fallen to the ground, and the bacterium *E. coli* can easily contaminate these fruits. If processors don't wash off this deadly bacterium before the apples are pressed, and the final product is not pasteurized, there is a risk of *E. coli* contamination, which can lead to severe health problems and even death. Although most bacteria cannot survive in the acidic conditions of vinegar, the acidity of the unpasteurized product can weaken over time, thus allowing bacteria to grow—and making the product dangerous for you.

To be on the safe side, be sure you always choose vinegars that have been prepared, pasteurized, and stored properly.

The quality of the original wine determines how good the vinegar is. Better wine vinegars are made from good wines and are aged for a couple of years or more in wooden casks. The result is a fuller, more complex, and mellow flavor.

You might find sherry vinegar on the shelf next to the wine vinegars. This variety is made from sherry wine and is usually imported from Spain. Champagne vinegar (yes, made from the bubbly stuff) is a specialty vinegar and is quite expensive.

Wine vinegar excels at bringing out the sweetness of fruit, melon, and berries and adds a flavorful punch to fresh salsa.

BALSAMIC VINEGAR

There are two types of this popular and delicious vinegar, traditional and commercial. A quasi-governmental body in Modena, Italy (balsamic vinegar's birthplace), regulates the production of traditional balsamic vinegar.

Traditional balsamic. Traditional balsamic vinegars are artisanal foods, similar to great wines, with long histories and well-developed customs for their production. An excellent balsamic vinegar can be made only by an experienced crafter who has spent many years tending the vinegar, patiently watching and learning.

The luscious white and sugary trebbiano grapes that are grown in the northern region of Italy near Modena form the base of the world's best and only true balsamic vinegars. Custom dictates that the grapes be left on the vine for as long as possible to develop their sugar. The juice (or "must") is pressed out of the grapes and boiled down; then, vinegar production begins.

Traditional balsamic vinegar is aged for a number of years—typically 6 and as many as 25. Aging takes place in a succession of casks made from a variety of woods, such as chestnut, mulberry, oak, juniper, and cherry. Each producer has its own formula for the order in which the vinegar is moved to the different casks. Thus, the flavors are complex, rich, sweet, and subtly woody. Vinegar made in this way carries a seal from the Consortium of Producers of the Traditional Balsamic Vinegar of Modena.

Because of the arduous production process, only a limited amount of traditional balsamic vinegar makes it to market each year, and what is available is expensive.

Leaf ratings. You might see that some traditional balsamic vinegars have leaves on their labels. This is a rating system that ranks quality on a one- to four-leaf scale, with four leaves being the best. You can use the leaf ranking as a guide for how to use the vinegar. For instance, one-leaf balsamic vinegar would be appropriate for salad dressing, while four-leaf vinegar would be best used a few drops at a time to season a dish right before serving. The

A TRIO OF FUNCTIONS

Vinegar is an invaluable kitchen staple that can be put to use in three important ways:

◆ It provides seasoning and a flavor boost.

◆ It acts as a preservative that can turn cucumbers and other summer vegetables into delicious pickles that can be safely stored for later use.

◆ It is useful in marinades to tenderize tough meat.

Assaggiatori Italiani Balsamico (Italian Balsamic Tasters' Association) established this grading system, but not all producers use it.

Commercial balsamic. What you're more likely to find in most American grocery stores is the commercial type of balsamic vinegar. Some is made in Modena, but not by traditional methods. In fact, some balsamic vinegar isn't even made in Italy. Commercial balsamic vinegar does not carry the Consortium of Producers of the Traditional Balsamic Vinegar of Modena seal because it is not produced in accordance with the Consortium's strict regulations.

The production of commercial balsamic vinegar carries no geographical restrictions or rules for length or method of aging. There are no requirements for the types of wood used in the aging casks. It may be aged for six months in stainless steel vats, then for two years or more in wood. Thus, commercial balsamic vinegar is much more affordable and available than the true, artisanal variety.

Whether you're lucky enough to get your hands on the traditional variety or you're using commercial-grade balsamic, the taste of this fine vinegar is like no other. Its sweet and sour notes are in perfect proportion. Balsamic's flavor is so intricate that it brings out the best in salty foods such as goat cheese, astringent foods such as spinach, and sweet foods such as strawberries.

RICE VINEGAR

Clear or very pale yellow, rice vinegar originated in Japan, where it is essential to sushi preparation. Rice vinegar is made from the sugars found in rice, and the aged, filtered final product has a mild, clean, and delicate flavor that is an excellent complement to ginger or cloves, sometimes with the addition of sugar.

Rice vinegar also comes in red and black varieties, which are not common in the United States but very popular in China. Both are stronger than the clear (often called white) or pale yellow types. Red rice vinegar's flavor is a combination of sweet and tart. Black rice vinegar is common in southern Chinese cooking and has a strong, almost smoky flavor.

Rice vinegar is popular in Asian cooking and is great sprinkled on salads and stir-fry dishes. Its gentle flavor is perfect for fruits and tender vegetables, too. Many cooks choose white rice vinegar for their recipes because it does not change the color of the food to which it is added. Red rice vinegar is good for soups and noodle dishes, and black rice vinegar works as a dipping sauce and in braised dishes.

MALT VINEGAR

This dark-brown vinegar, a favorite in Britain, is reminiscent of deep-brown ale. Malt vinegar production begins with the germination, or sprouting, of barley kernels. Germination enables enzymes to break down starch into sugar. The resulting product is brewed into an alcohol-containing malt beverage or ale. After bacteria convert the ale to vinegar, the vinegar is aged. As its name implies, malt vinegar has a distinctive malt flavor.

A cheaper and less flavorful version of malt vinegar consists merely of acetic acid diluted to between 4 percent and 8 percent acidity, with a little caramel coloring added.

Many people prefer malt vinegar for pickling and as an accompaniment to fish and chips. It is also used as the basic type of cooking vinegar in Britain.

CANE VINEGAR

This type of vinegar is produced from the sugar cane and is used mainly in the Philippines. It is often light yellow and has a flavor similar to rice vinegar. Contrary to what you might think, cane vinegar is not any sweeter than other vinegars.

LAST-MINUTE SPLASH

Vinegar loses some of its pungency when heated. If you want to enjoy vinegar's full tart taste, add it to a dish at the end of cooking. Also, after heating up leftovers, splash them with vinegar to perk up their flavors.

BEER VINEGAR

Beer vinegar has an appealing light-golden color and, as you might guess, is popular in Germany, Austria, Bavaria, and the Netherlands. It is made from beer, and its flavor depends on the brew from which it was made. It has a sharp, malty taste.

COCONUT VINEGAR

If you can't get your Asian recipes to taste "just right," it might be because you don't have coconut vinegar—a white vinegar with a sharp, acidic, slightly yeasty taste. This staple of Southeast Asian cooking is made from the sap of the coconut palm and is especially important to Thai and Indian dishes.

Raisin Vinegar

This slightly cloudy, brown vinegar is traditionally produced in Turkey and used in Middle Eastern cuisines. Try infusing it with a little cinnamon to bolster its mild flavor. Salad dressings made with raisin vinegar will add an unconventional taste to your greens.

Make Your Own Apple Cider Vinegar

Perhaps reading about all these exciting kinds of vinegar has whetted your appetite to make some of your own. Experimenting with flavors can be fun, and it's especially rewarding to use your own vinegar in your favorite dishes or to give it as a gift.

You'll want to get exact directions from your local brewing supply store or university extension service. Be sure the directions you follow are tested and researched for safety to avoid food-borne illness. Take a look at this rundown of the general process to make apple cider vinegar to see if you're up to the task:

◆ Make apple cider by pressing clean, washed, ripe apples (fall apples have more sugar than early-season apples). Strain to make a clean juice and pour it into sterilized containers.

◆ Use yeast designed for brewing wine or beer (not baker's yeast) to ferment the fruit sugar into alcohol.

◆ Now let bacteria convert the alcohol to acetic acid. Leaving the fermenting liquid uncovered invites acid-making bacteria to take up residence. (You might, however, want to place some cheesecloth or a towel over your container's opening to prevent insects, dirt, or other nasty items from

ALL ABOUT ACIDITY

The U.S. Food and Drug Administration requires that vinegar contain a minimum of 4 percent acetic acid. White vinegar is typically 5 percent acetic acid, and cider and wine vinegars are a bit more acidic, usually between 5 percent and 6 percent.

A little acidity goes a long way—acetic acid is corrosive and can destroy living tissues when concentrated. An acetic acid level of 11 percent or more can burn the skin. And according to the Consumer Product Safety Commission, an "acetic acid preparation containing free or chemically unneutralized acetic acid in a concentration of 20 percent or more" is considered poison. In fact, a 20 percent acetic acid concentration is sometimes used as an herbicide to kill garden weeds.

getting into the mixture.) Some vinegar brewers use a "mother of vinegar" (see box, page 40) as a "starter," or source of the acid-producing bacteria.

◆ Keep the liquid between 60 degrees and 80 degrees Fahrenheit during the fermentation process; it will take three to four weeks to make vinegar. If you keep the liquid too cool, the vinegar may be unusable. If it's kept too warm, it may not form the mother of vinegar mat at the bottom of the container. The mother of vinegar mat signifies proper fermentation. Stir the liquid daily to introduce adequate amounts of oxygen, which is necessary for fermentation.

MOTHER OF VINEGAR

If you see a jellylike cloudy film collecting in the bottom of your vinegar bottle, you've discovered the "mother of vinegar." It's merely cellulose made by acid-producing bacteria. Mother of vinegar is a completely natural by-product of vinegar that contains live bacteria. It is harmless and is not a sign of contamination. Just strain off the liquid vinegar and continue using it.

Most manufacturers pasteurize their vinegar to prevent mother of vinegar from forming. Some say this goo prevents infectious diseases if you eat a little each day, but there is no research to verify that belief.

* After three to four weeks, the bacteria will have converted most of the alcohol, and the mixture will begin to smell like vinegar. Taste a little bit each day until it reaches a flavor and acidity that you like.

* Strain the liquid through a cheesecloth or coffee filter several times to remove the mother of vinegar. Otherwise the fermentation process will continue and eventually spoil your vinegar.

* Store in sterilized, capped jars in the refrigerator.

* If you want to store homemade vinegar at room temperature for more than a few months, you must pasteurize it. Do this by heating it to 170 degrees Fahrenheit (use a cooking thermometer to determine the temperature) and hold it at this temperature for 10 minutes. Put the pasteurized vinegar in sterilized containers with tight-fitting lids, out of direct sunlight.

FLAVOR INFUSION

Whether you start with homemade or store-bought vinegar, you can kick it up by adding flavorful herbs or spices. Garlic, basil, rosemary, and tarragon are herbs commonly added to white wine vinegar. Other herbs or fruits, such as raspberries, also can enhance vinegar's taste. These additions leave their flavors and trace amounts of healthy nutrients, too.

Herbal vinegars need to be carefully prepared to avoid contamination with potentially harmful bacteria. Most bacteria cannot exist in vinegar's acidic environment, but a few deadly ones can, so follow these basic steps:

- Use only high-quality vinegars when creating flavor combinations. Typically, white wine vinegar or red wine vinegar are best for flavoring. Remember, though, that these vinegars contain trace amounts of protein that could give harmful bacteria an ideal place to live unless you prepare and store the vinegars properly.

- Wash your storage bottles and then sterilize them by completely immersing them in boiling water for 10 minutes. Always fill the bottles while they are still warm, and be sure you have a tight-fitting lid, cap, or cork for each one.

- If you're using fresh herbs, there is a risk of harmful bacteria hitchhiking their way into the vinegar via the sprigs. Commercial vinegar processors use antimicrobial agents to sanitize herbs, but you probably won't be able to find these chemicals. University extension publications recommend mixing one teaspoon of bleach into six cups of water and dipping the fresh herbs into this solution. Then rinse the herbs thoroughly and pat them dry. This will minimize the possibility of any harmful bacteria making their way into the vinegar and will not affect the taste.

♦ Be sure your fresh herbs are in top-notch condition—bruising or decay indicates the presence of bacteria. If you harvest your own herbs, do so in the morning, when the essential oils are at their peak. Use three to four sprigs or three tablespoons of dried herbs per pint of vinegar. Mix it up a bit by adding some spices or vegetables, such as garlic or hot peppers. Thread garlic, peppers, or other small items on a skewer so you can remove them easily when you've infused enough flavor.

♦ To add fruit flavors to vinegar, thoroughly wash fruit, berries, or citrus rind. Use one to two cups of fruit for every pint of vinegar, but only the rind of one lemon or orange per pint. You can thread small fruits or chunks of fruit on a skewer and tie chopped rind in a small piece of clean cheesecloth to make removal easy.

♦ When you're ready to start mixing, place the herbs or flavoring in the sterilized, hot bottles. Heat the vinegar to 190 degrees Fahrenheit and then pour it over the herbs in the sterilized bottles. Heating the vinegar to 190 degrees Fahrenheit will prevent bacteria from forming and also help release the essential oils from the herbs, spices, or fruits.

♦ Put a tight-fitting lid on your container and allow the vinegar to stand in a cool, dark place for three to four weeks. When it has enough flavor, strain it through a cheesecloth or coffee filter several times until any cloudiness is gone.

♦ Discard the fruits, spices, or herbs and pour the filtered vinegar into newly sterilized containers. If you want to add a decorative herb sprig, sanitize it using the method described on page 41. Seal tightly.

◆ Store the vinegar in the refrigerator for the best flavor retention; it will keep well for six to eight months. Unrefrigerated vinegar will keep its flavor for only two to three months. If the bottle has been left to look pretty on a sunny windowsill for more than a few weeks, use the vinegar only as decoration, not as food.

◆ You can use your herbal vinegar in nearly any recipe that calls for plain vinegar.

VINEGAR MAGIC

Storing vinegar properly will hold flavor at its peak. Due to their high acid content, commercially prepared vinegars will keep almost indefinitely, even at room temperature. White vinegar will maintain its color, but other kinds may develop an off color or a haze. Neither of these conditions is a sign of spoilage; the vinegar is still good to use.

A HOMEMADE-VINEGAR CAUTION

The acidity of homemade vinegar varies greatly. If you make your own vinegar, *do not* use it for canning, for preserving, or for anything that will be stored at room temperature. The vinegar's acidity, or pH level, may not be sufficient to preserve your food and could result in severe food poisoning. The pH level in homemade vinegar can weaken and allow pathogens, such as the deadly *E. coli*, to grow. Homemade vinegar is well suited for dressings, marinades, cooking, or pickled products that are stored in the refrigerator at all times.

Store all vinegars in bottles sealed with airtight lids. Keep in a dark, cool place, and avoid direct sunlight, which can diminish flavor, color, and acidity. Homemade vinegars, especially herbal ones, are best stored in the refrigerator.

Vinegar's acidity makes it a natural wonder in your kitchen. Besides the burst of flavor vinegar lends to whatever it touches, it serves other purposes, including the following:

◆ *Meat tenderizer:* Vinegar's acid helps break down muscle fibers in tough meats. Make a mixture of half vinegar and half broth, and soak tough meat in this solution for up to two hours. (Because of vinegar's ability to tenderize, never leave fish in a marinade that contains vinegar for longer than 20 minutes; otherwise the fish might get mushy.)

THE BETTER OF TWO WORLDS

Vinegar is good for you, and garlic is great. Why not combine the two and make pickled garlic? Simply peel some garlic cloves, cube them, and let them sit for 10 to 15 minutes to form allicin, a powerful sulfur-containing agent that helps protect your body's cells from damage. Then add the garlic to your favorite vinegar.

Vinegar helps garlic form healthful sulfur-containing compounds that are not otherwise formed in large amounts. The longer the garlic is in the vinegar, the more sulfur compounds it forms. Store your pickled garlic in the refrigerator and add it to salads and vegetable side dishes. What a delicious way to take your medicine—maybe a pickled clove a day will keep the doctor away.

♦ *Fish poacher:* When poaching fish, put a tablespoon of vinegar in the poaching water to keep the fish from falling apart. Vinegar helps the protein in the fish coagulate, and mushiness isn't a problem because fish is usually poached for less than 20 minutes.

♦ *Egg saver:* Put a tablespoon of vinegar in the water when boiling eggs. If any eggs crack while dancing in the water, their whites will coagulate so they can't escape from the shells.

♦ *Buttermilk stand-in:* When a recipe calls for buttermilk and you have none, substitute plain milk and add a little vinegar. Use one tablespoon of vinegar per cup (eight ounces) of milk. Let stand 10 to 15 minutes at room temperature until it thickens, then use it in your recipe as you would buttermilk. Choose mild-flavored vinegar, such as apple cider vinegar, for this purpose.

♦ *Lemon and lime substitute:* Vinegar can be used in any recipe calling for lemon or lime juice. Use a half teaspoon vinegar for each teaspoon of lemon or lime.

♦ *Candy smoother:* When making homemade candy and icing, a few drops of vinegar will prevent the texture from getting grainy.

♦ *Potato whitener:* Cover peeled potatoes with water and a tablespoon or two of vinegar to keep them from browning.

♦ *Food preserver:* Use vinegar to make pickles or to can vegetables to preserve the freshness of your garden or local farm stand. The U.S. Department of Agriculture (USDA) publishes up-to-date information about pickling, canning, and preserving. These instructions will yield tasty pickles and home-canned products that are safe to eat. Check your local state university extension office or the USDA Web site (www.usda.gov) for tips about pickling.

PERK UP RECIPES

Vinegar adds zip to the most mundane meals. And it doesn't take much to liven foods up. If you add a drop here and there during the preparation process, vinegar may even change the whole personality of certain foods. Here are some ideas for improving your recipes:

◆ For a more flavorful burger, add garlic wine vinegar and a half teaspoon mustard to a pound of ground meat. Work the ingredients into the meat before making patties.

◆ Improve the flavor of boiled ham by adding one tablespoon vinegar to cooking water.

◆ In a tomato sauce or a tomato-based soup, add one or two tablespoons vinegar just before completing the cooking process. Flavors will be enhanced.

◆ Add a tablespoon or more of vinegar when frying or boiling fish to reduce fishy tastes and smells and to keep the meat soft.

◆ Give canned shrimp and fish a freshly caught taste by covering it in sherry and adding two tablespoons vinegar. Soak for 15 minutes, then prepare as desired.

◆ When cooking fruit on the stovetop, add a spoonful of vinegar to improve flavor.

◆ **Bread riser:** You can help make homemade bread rise by adding one tablespoon vinegar for every two-and-a-half cups flour in the recipe. Reduce other liquids in the recipe appropriately.

◆ **Wine substitute:** If you mix vinegar with water first, you can substitute it for wine in any recipe. Mix a ratio of one part vinegar to three parts water, then use whatever amount your recipe calls for in place of wine.

◆ **Cheese protector:** Wrap leftover hard cheese in a cloth saturated with vinegar, then store in an airtight container. This will keep cheese from molding or becoming too hard.

◆ **Veggie freshener:** Freshen wilted vegetables such as spinach or lettuce by soaking them in two cups water and one tablespoon vinegar.

◆ **Meringue fluffer:** Make a fluffier meringue that is also more stable by adding vinegar to egg whites before beating. For every three egg whites in the recipe, add a half teaspoon vinegar.

◆ **Bread browner:** Make the crust of homemade bread a nice, golden brown by removing it from the oven shortly before the baking time is complete and brushing it with vinegar. Return to oven to finish baking.

VINEGAR'S VIM

No matter how you look at it, vinegar can add spice to your culinary life. Prowl the gourmet shops in your area and you'll find dozens of different vinegars. Select a few to bring home to try, using the ideas in this book. Your taste buds will definitely be pleased, but it may be your health that benefits most.

Vinegar to the Rescue!

Let vinegar solve some common, frustrating household problems:

- Pour about a teaspoon of vinegar into a nearly empty mayonnaise jar and swish it around to get out the last of the mayonnaise.

- Use it to remove berry stains from your hands.

- Soak a paper towel with vinegar and place it in a smelly lunchbox overnight to remove those hard-to-get-rid-of odors.

- Simmer a small saucepan of water and vinegar to remove cooking smells from the kitchen.

- A mixture of equal parts vinegar, salt, and baking soda may help open up a slow-draining sink. Pour solution down drain, let sit an hour, then pour boiling or very hot tap water down the drain.

- Prevent mildew buildup inside your refrigerator or on its rubber seals by wiping occasionally with a sponge dampened with undiluted vinegar. No need to rinse.

- Add vinegar to a piecrust recipe and the dough will be easier to roll out. (The crust may be less flaky, however.) Most recipes call for about a tablespoon of vinegar for a double crust.

- If your microwave is spattered with old sauces and greasy buildup, place a glass measuring cup containing one cup water and a quarter cup vinegar inside it. Boil for three minutes, then remove measuring cup and wipe inside of oven with a damp sponge.